W is for Welcome

A Celebration of America's Diversity

Written by Brad Herzog

Illustrated by a collection of nationally acclaimed artists

Each year, millions of people leave their homelands to start new lives in another country. They emigrate *from* their birth nation and immigrate *to* a new one. America, in particular, is made up of immigrants and their descendants. Everyone is here because their ancestors once "migrated" (moved from one place to another). Some of them, such as the ancestors of Native Americans, migrated to North America very long ago. Many others arrived against their will. For instance, hundreds of thousands of Africans were forced to come here and were enslaved. But over the centuries, the United States has welcomed millions of strangers to its shores.

Illustrated by Pam Carroll

A is for America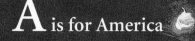

A is for America,
a dreamer's destination,
made up of people who are here
due to immigration.

B is for the Bering Strait

Thousands of years ago,
  these waters were once spanned
by an invitation to explore—
  a narrow bridge of land.

Way up north, near the Arctic Circle, the continents of Asia and North America are less than 60 miles apart. The narrow sea passage between them is called the Bering Strait. Thousands of years ago, water levels there were lower than they are now. Scientists believe this exposed a bridge of land connecting the two continents. That land allowed early humans to migrate into what is now Alaska.

Historians currently believe these were the first people in North America and were the ancestors of many Native Americans and of Canada's First Nations people.

Illustrated by Michael Glenn Monroe

C c

C is for Cultures

A salad bowl of many flavors.
A multicolored quilt.
A marvelous mix of everything
is the country that we've built.

A culture is the collective beliefs, customs, and achievements of any group of people. Bringing together so many people from so many places has made the United States an amazing blend of cultures. Often, something that we might think of as being very American was actually created by people from somewhere else. The banjo and similar instruments were brought to North America from West Africa. Blue jeans were created for California miners by an immigrant from Bavaria named Levi Strauss. Even basketball was invented in Massachusetts by a Canadian immigrant, James Naismith.

This is true for some Americans' favorite foods, too. The hot dog was created by a German immigrant who placed a sausage in a sliced roll. Apple pie came from recipes in England long ago. And an Italian immigrant, Gennaro Lombardi, opened America's first pizzeria in 1905.

D is for Diversity

People from every land,
  all religions and all races,
form a picture showing
  so many different faces.

About 80 million people in the United States either were born in other countries or are the children of immigrants. One example of America's diversity is the small city of Clarkston, Georgia. In 1980, nearly every person in Clarkston had been born in America. But in the 1990s the city decided to welcome refugees from around the world. Refugees are people fleeing a natural disaster, war, violence, or severe mistreatment due to their race, religion, or political beliefs.

As a result, *Time* magazine called Clarkston the nation's "most diverse square mile." Only about 7,500 people live there, but nearly one-third of them are immigrants from Vietnam, Bhutan, Iraq, Somalia, Syria, and about 40 other countries.

Illustrated by Laura Knorr

Dd

E e

E is for Ellis Island

Millions of immigrants
full of hopes and fears
arrived there by ship
over more than 60 years.

Ellis Island is located in Upper New York Bay near the Statue of Liberty. From 1892 to 1954, it was an inspection station and the first stop for nearly 12 million immigrants. In fact, nearly half of all U.S. citizens have ancestors who passed through there. The very first was seventeen-year-old Annie Moore from Ireland. Today, a statue of Annie stands at the Ellis Island National Museum of Immigration.

The "Ellis Island of the West" was the Angel Island Immigration Station in San Francisco Bay. Nearly one million immigrants from Asia arrived there between 1910 and 1940. However, laws like the Chinese Exclusion Act of 1882 and the Immigration Act of 1924 actually prevented most immigrants from Asia from entering the United States. Many thousands of people who dreamed of a better life were detained at Angel Island, sometimes for years.

F is for Freedom

Worship as you wish.
Speak out. Protest. Feel free.
So many people come here
for that opportunity.

In a famous speech in 1941, President Franklin D. Roosevelt spoke about four freedoms he said people "everywhere in the world" deserve: freedom of speech, freedom of worship, freedom from want, and freedom from fear. Many immigrants come from countries where they have not been able to freely express their ideas and are not free from daily violence or hunger. They cannot practice their chosen religion (or practice no religion at all). Many of the freedoms that Americans enjoy are stated in the Bill of Rights, the first ten amendments to the U.S. Constitution.

Illustrated by Pam Carroll

Ff

G is for "God Bless America"
Irving Berlin was born in Russia,
but crossed an ocean "white with foam"
and wrote a song to celebrate
his beloved "home sweet home."

Five-year-old Israel Beilin (changed to Baline at Ellis Island) immigrated to the United States in 1893. He and his parents came here because Jewish families in Russia were persecuted. He worked as a street singer in New York City and began composing songs in his late teens. As a young man, he changed his name to Berlin.

By the time he died at age 101, Irving Berlin was known worldwide as one of the greatest songwriters in American history. Berlin wrote "God Bless America," which was first performed in 1938. It was his way of thanking the country that welcomed him. Berlin donated the millions of dollars he earned from the song to the New York City area chapters of the Boy Scouts and Girl Scouts of America.

Illustrated by David C. Gardner

H is for Heroes

A whole nation cheers wildly
for the U.S. Olympic team
and many athletes born elsewhere
who achieve an American dream.

There are many kinds of heroes. Sometimes even athletes make heroic journeys just for a chance to compete. As a young boy in war-torn Sudan, Lopez Lomong was kidnapped by soldiers but soon escaped and made his way to a refugee camp in Kenya. Years later, he and several thousand other "lost boys" of Sudan's civil war were brought to America. Lomong became a U.S. citizen and a track star. In 2008, he competed at the Summer Olympics and carried the American flag during the opening ceremony.

Over the years, there have been many U.S. Olympians who were born elsewhere. Forty-seven such athletes competed in the 2016 Summer Games. Some even won gold medals (hurdler Kerron Clement from Trinidad and Tobago), silver medals (gymnast Danell Leyva from Cuba), and bronze medals (fencer Dagmara Wozniak from Poland).

Illustrated by Doug Bowles

Ii

I is for Immigration

> From Italy to India,
> most everywhere on Earth,
> are people who have moved away
> from their place of birth.

A migrant is a person living in a country that is different from his or her place of birth. About one of every seven U.S. residents has come from another country. But immigration happens all around the world.

In fact, there are nearly 250 million immigrants in nations around the globe. A dozen countries each have a population of at least five million immigrants—the United States, the United Kingdom, the United Arab Emirates, Saudi Arabia, Canada, Australia, Russia, Germany, Spain, France, Italy, and India.

Illustrated by Laura Knorr

Most immigrants today arrive in the United States by airplane. It is a long way from a century ago when millions braved an often long, stormy voyage aboard steamships. They crowded into narrow bunks belowdecks where there was little fresh air. Many arrived with barely more than the clothes they were wearing.

But many refugees and undocumented immigrants (people who cross a border in a way that violates the immigration laws of the country) still face dangerous journeys. They may risk their lives trekking through the desert on foot, climbing aboard slow-moving freight trains, or riding atop rickety rafts across the Gulf of Mexico. That's how desperate they are to reach America.

Illustrated by

Gijsbert van Frankenhuyzen

J is for Journey

So many ways to come here—
    by foot, by air, by sea.
A long trip to America,
    hoping for liberty.

K is for Knowledge

From all over the globe,
   in a quest to know much more,
brilliant thinkers come here
   and continue to explore.

EINSTEIN

Many great geniuses became American citizens after emigrating from other countries. Nikola Tesla was born in what is now Croatia. He became a celebrated inventor in New York City. Men like Albert Einstein (from Germany) and women like Chien-Shiung Wu (from China) are legendary scientists. Scottish immigrant Andrew Carnegie became one of the wealthiest men in America. Then he used much of his fortune to establish hundreds of libraries.

U.S. immigrants have explored space, too. José Hernández was the son of Mexican migrant farmworkers. He didn't learn to speak English until he was 12. At age 41, he became a U.S. astronaut.

Illustrated by Renée Graef

L is for Lady Liberty

This special gift from France
is a lasting symbol of
a welcome to the world
and the freedoms that we love.

The 151-foot-tall Statue of Liberty was dedicated in 1886. This gift to the United States was mostly paid for by the people of France, including thousands of French schoolchildren. It was transported in pieces to its location on Liberty Island in New York Harbor. Liberty Enlightening the World (its official name) was built by Gustave Eiffel, who also constructed the Eiffel Tower in Paris. It was designed by French sculptor Frédéric-Auguste Bartholdi. Although the copper statue represents the Roman goddess Libertas, Bartholdi actually may have used his mother as a model!

The statue stands on a huge pedestal that was paid for by donations from thousands of Americans. The man who largely made that happen was newspaper publisher Joseph Pulitzer. He had emigrated from Hungary as a teenager.

Illustrated by Pam Carroll

L l

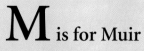

M is for Muir

Scottish immigrant John Muir
saw the devastation
of America's natural wonders
and called for conservation.

Conservation is an effort to preserve and protect a place of great natural beauty and importance. Our national parks preserve our country's most magnificent places. That's why they have been called our greatest treasures.

Although he wasn't responsible for creating the first one, John Muir has been called "the Father of the National Parks." After emigrating from Scotland, Muir spent much of his life exploring America. He wrote books and articles about the importance of enjoying and protecting natural wonders. Muir walked thousands of miles across fields, forests, and mountains, including his favorite spot, Yosemite Valley. He played an important role in the creation of Yosemite National Park. President Theodore Roosevelt joined Muir on a camping trip in Yosemite in 1903. Afterward, the president became a dedicated conservationist, too.

Illustrated by Pam Carroll

If a citizen of a foreign country wishes to become a lawful permanent resident of the United States, the first step is usually to obtain an immigrant visa. This is stamped in a passport and allows the visitor to be in the United States for a certain amount of time. A permanent resident receives a plastic photo ID card called a "green card."

Through a legal process known as naturalization, foreign citizens can apply to become U.S. citizens if they are over age 18 and have been lawful permanent residents for at least five years. After completing an application, they must get fingerprinted and attend an interview. They must also pass both an English test and a test examining their understanding of U.S. history and government. As U.S. citizens, they can then vote in public elections and be protected from deportation (removal from the country).

N is for Naturalization

Thousands of immigrants
who live and work hard here
are naturalized and become
U.S. citizens each year.

O is for Oath

New citizens pledge to accept
an important obligation—
to support and defend the laws
of their adopted nation.

O o

People who wished to be American citizens have taken an oath to support the U.S. Constitution since way back in 1790. The Oath of Allegiance is the last step in the naturalization process. Immigrants from many countries take part in a large public ceremony. They raise their right hands, swear loyalty to the United States, and promise to defend the nation when required by law. This is usually followed by cheering and waving of tiny American flags. They are then handed Certificates of Naturalization as U.S. citizens.

Illustrated by Victor Juhasz

P is for Poem

A "world-wide welcome" states,
"Give me your tired, your poor."
And then it adds, "I lift my lamp
beside the golden door!"

In 1883, poet Emma Lazarus was asked to write a poem. She was told it would help raise money for building the Statue of Liberty's huge pedestal (see letter L). So Lazarus wrote "The New Colossus." It was a sonnet about "a mighty woman with a torch" who offered freedom and comfort to immigrants.

When Lazarus died only four years later, at age 38, the poem was largely forgotten. But in 1903, it was engraved on a bronze tablet that was placed inside the pedestal. Her beautiful words have since come to define America's long tradition of welcoming immigrants.

Illustrated by Doug Bowles

The New Colossus

People from around the world may decide to move to America to find jobs that allow them to live more comfortably. Perhaps they seek freedom of speech and religion. Maybe they wish to reunite with family already living in the United States. They may immigrate out of a sense of hope or adventure. Or they may be desperate to leave terrible difficulties, such as war or civil strife, behind. Immigrants want to make a better life for themselves and their children. Whatever the reasons, it requires courage to start a new life in an unfamiliar place.

Illustrated by Victor Juhasz

Q is for Quest

A chance to seek a better life.
Join family. Work and thrive.
There are countless reasons why
immigrants arrive.

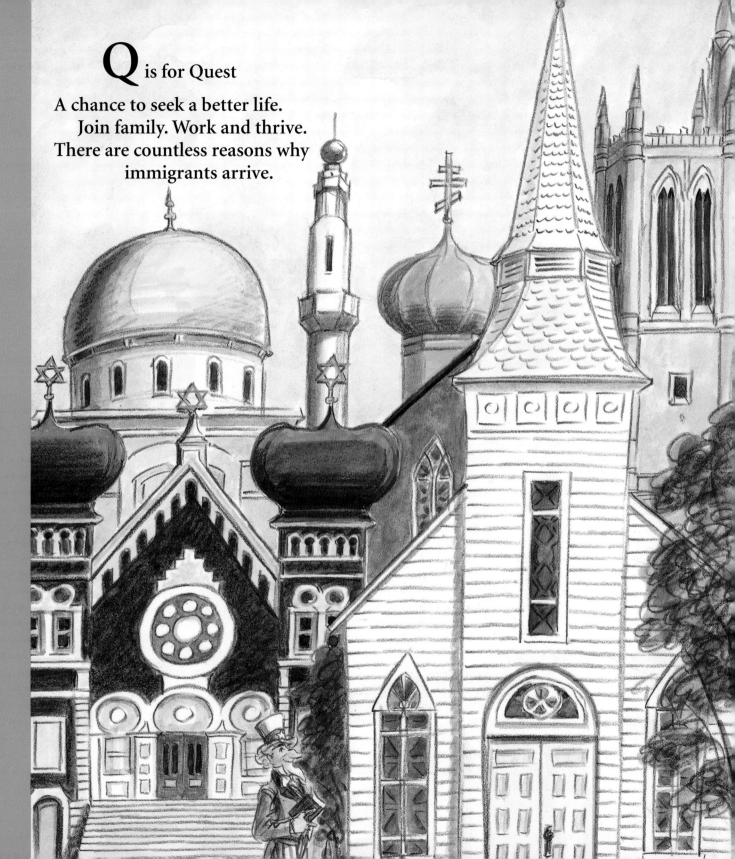

R is for Refugees

Many people leave their country for the U.S. or other nations because they're desperate to escape dangerous situations.

Refugees are people who have been forced to leave their country and cannot return home safely. There are millions of them around the world—and there have been for hundreds of years.

They may face starvation, like Irish immigrants who fled the Great Famine after potato crops failed in the mid-nineteenth century. They may wish to escape horrific treatment, like Jewish refugees from Nazi Germany in the twentieth century. Or they may be fleeing from violent civil wars such as those in Sudan and Syria in the twenty-first century. International laws protect refugees from being returned to situations that risk their freedom or their lives.

Illustrated by Victor Juhasz

More than one out of every ten U.S. military veterans is an immigrant or the child of immigrants. Hundreds of foreign-born members of the U.S. military have received medals for courage in action (including the Medal of Honor). Hundreds also have been killed in action, sacrificing their lives for their new country.

Public service is another way of giving back. Madeleine Albright, the first female U.S. Secretary of State, was born in Czechoslovakia. She came to America in 1948. About a decade later, a man from Kenya arrived in the United States to attend college. He married a woman from Kansas, and they had a son—future president Barack Obama.

Illustrated by Victor Juhasz

S s

S is for Service

How best to show thanks
for being a U.S. citizen?
By giving back to the place
that said to them, "Come in!"

T is for Transcontinental Railroad

Chinese and Irish immigrants
 were the workers who did most
to build the first train tracks
 that stretched from coast to coast.

In 1862, the federal government decided to build a "transcontinental" railroad, one that would link the nation from east to west. The Union Pacific Railroad laid tracks moving westward from the Missouri River, relying mostly on Irish immigrant workers. Meanwhile, the Central Pacific Railroad moved eastward from California. Most of its laborers came from China. It was dangerous work, as they often had to blast tunnels through mountains.

Finally, after laying nearly 1,800 miles of track, the two railroads met at Promontory, Utah, on May 10, 1869. Americans could now more easily travel from coast to coast, thanks in part to tireless workers from other countries.

Illustrated by Susan Guy

An immigrant's face is on the ten-dollar bill. Alexander Hamilton was born about 1755 on the Caribbean island of Nevis. At age 17, he moved to New York City to attend school. Just a few years later, he was General George Washington's chief assistant during the Revolutionary War. As one of America's Founding Fathers, Hamilton created the first national bank and served as the first secretary of the treasury.

More than 200 years later, his story was celebrated in the hip-hop musical *Hamilton*, created by Lin-Manuel Miranda. Miranda's ancestors include an early white American, a black slave, and residents of Puerto Rico, located not far from Hamilton's birthplace.

Illustrated by Laura Knorr

U is for United States

One of the youngest Founding Fathers
on the revolutionary scene,
Alexander Hamilton moved here
when he was just a teen.

U u

V V

V is for Voices

Each immigrant has a tale to tell
about how and why they came
to live in the United States.
No two stories are the same.

When I first saw the Statue of Liberty, I cried tears of joy.

This is the land of great opportunity

We had nothing when we arrived but a shirt on our

I was a young man when I arrived and now

The best way to understand how and why immigrants journeyed to America is by examining their own words. The Ellis Island Oral History project has gathered about 2,000 interviews with people who passed through there many decades ago. And students at the University of Maryland are collecting the memories of modern-day immigrants from Albania, Malaysia, Venezuela, and many other places in its Archive of Immigrant Voices. There are also a great many books that tell specific tales or gather together stories told by various immigrants.

Illustrated by Ross B. Young

W is for the White House

Only in America,
land of opportunity,
could an Irishman design the jewel
of Washington, D.C.

Every president except George Washington has lived at America's most famous address—1600 Pennsylvania Avenue. But the architect of the White House was born and trained in Ireland. James Hoban immigrated to the United States in 1785. Seven years later, he was asked to design the presidential mansion. He worked closely with President Washington on its creation. Hoban also recruited stonemasons from Scotland to quarry the stone for the building.

It is important to note that enslaved people worked to build the White House, too. So while its builders were a diverse group, the country still had a very long way to go.

Illustrated by Barbara Gibson

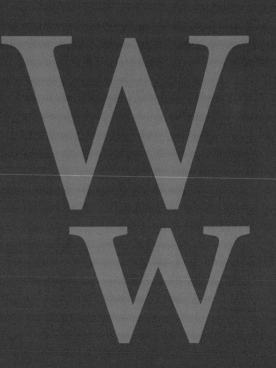

X is for X Marks the Spot

At Plymouth Rock, the Pilgrims landed
after braving stormy seas.
They came to a New World
as its first refugees.

In autumn 1620, about 100 men and women set sail from England aboard a ship known as the *Mayflower*. They were fleeing because the Church of England would not allow them to worship as they wished. After a two-month voyage across the Atlantic Ocean, they formed the Plymouth Colony in what is now Massachusetts. These brave religious dissenters became known many years later as the Pilgrims. A pilgrim is a traveler who seeks a sacred place. Their sacred place was a new land offering religious freedom.

Illustrated by Helle Urban

Jawed Karim's father emigrated from Bangladesh. He met Jawed's mother in Germany. When Jawed was 13, the family moved to Saint Paul, Minnesota. In 2005, Jawed and friends Chad Hurley and Steve Chen created YouTube. In fact, Jawed uploaded the first video—a 19-second clip of himself standing in front of elephants at a zoo. His YouTube partner Steve Chen grew up in Taiwan before moving to Illinois.

U.S. immigrants also co-created Internet companies such as Google and Yahoo! And let's not forget Ralph Baer. He emigrated from Germany in 1938. About 30 years later, he invented the first home video game console.

Illustrated by Renée Graef

Y is for YouTube

Turn on your computer.
Watch a video.
Two immigrants to the U.S.
helped to make it so.

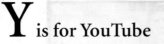

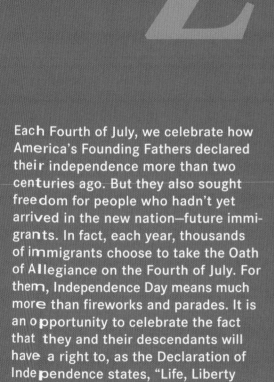

Zz

Each Fourth of July, we celebrate how America's Founding Fathers declared their independence more than two centuries ago. But they also sought freedom for people who hadn't yet arrived in the new nation—future immigrants. In fact, each year, thousands of immigrants choose to take the Oath of Allegiance on the Fourth of July. For them, Independence Day means much more than fireworks and parades. It is an opportunity to celebrate the fact that they and their descendants will have a right to, as the Declaration of Independence states, "Life, Liberty and the pursuit of Happiness."

It is also a reminder that the first seven words of the U.S. Constitution—"We the People of the United States"—mean people of all kinds, from all places.

Illustrated by Maureen K. Brookfield

Z is for Zeal

On Independence Day,
we all can celebrate
how people of all stripes (and stars)
have made this country great.

To my great-grandparents and great-great-grandparents, who immigrated to America in the nineteenth century from various places in Central Europe. And to anyone who has had the courage to seek refuge, opportunity, freedom, or family in a foreign land.
—Brad

⚬◦⚬

Sleeping Bear Press wishes to thank Thomas Collier (retired lecturer in history, University of Michigan) and Mary Byatt (educator at Birches School, Turnersville, New Jersey) for their reading of the manuscript and for offering insightful feedback.

Sleeping Bear Press®

2395 South Huron Parkway, Suite 200
Ann Arbor, MI 48104
www.sleepingbearpress.com

Printed and bound in the United States.

Library of Congress Cataloging-in-Publication Data

Names: Herzog, Brad, author.
Title: W is for welcome : a celebration of America's diversity / written by
Brad Herzog ; illustrated by a collection of nationally acclaimed artists.
Description: Ann Arbor, MI : Sleeping Bear Press, 2018.
Identifiers: LCCN 2017029875 | ISBN 9781585364022
Subjects: LCSH: Cultural pluralism--United States--Juvenile literature.
| Immigrants--United States--Juvenile literature. | United States--Race
relations--Juvenile literature. | United States--Ethnic
relations--Juvenile literature. | Alphabet books--Juvenile literature.
Classification: LCC E184.A1 H476 2018 | DDC 305.800973--dc23
LC record available at https://lccn.loc.gov/2017029875